Walking in the Welsh borders:

The Borderlands

This is fine country, offering famous moun[t ...]
waterways, the Forest of Dean, and a good [...]
the finest venue for walkers of all abilities.
These so called *'Disputed territories'* have at times been [...]
but the hills, the rivers and the farm just go on down through the centuries ignoring it all.

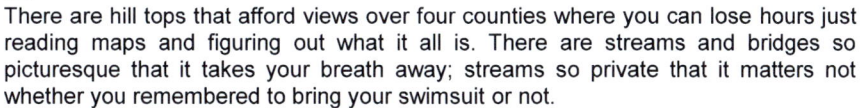

There are hill tops that afford views over four counties where you can lose hours just reading maps and figuring out what it all is. There are streams and bridges so picturesque that it takes your breath away; streams so private that it matters not whether you remembered to bring your swimsuit or not.

There are paths that wander between forests and meandering streams where we can find animals and plants of endless variety.

There is a village pub adjacent to every walk that will offer the best in open fires, home cooking, fine wines and excellent real ales. We'll recommend at least one for each walk.

There are people; and they're quite pleasant, too. Buy them a drink and they might even feign interest in your walking tales.

Contents

Walking in the Welsh borders: 1
   The Borderlands 1
   On walking guides… 2
   On litter… 2
   On safety… 2
   And health… 3
   On paths… 3
   On equipment… 4
   Places to visit 5
Llancloudy to Llangrove (*and the fabulous Royal Arms*) 6
Coppett Hill 9
Coppett Hill, shorter alternative 12
Garway Hill 14
Symonds Yat 17
The Three Castles Walk 19
The 3-Castles: Step one: White castle to Grosmont Castle 19
   Perhaps a note from your Mother would help? 21
The 3-Castles: Step Two: Grosmont Castle to Skenfrith Castle. 22
   Incidentally, thank you for buying this book of walks, but… 24
The 3-Castles: Step Three: Skenfrith Castle to White Castle. 26
   How did this all start? 27
Llanthony Priory 28
   Troubles 30
The Sugarloaf Mountain, from Abergavenny; shortest route. 31
The Sugarloaf Mountain, from Abergavenny, longer, circular route 34
Little Skirrid Mountain from Abergavenny circuit 37
   We'll enjoy this beer; we only did the short route! Hurrah!! 41
The Kymin, Monmouth longer walk 42

On walking guides…

Walking guides come in many forms, and it is *'horses for courses'*. Some are written by professional writers who have been granted enough expenses for a week in a location and write excellent prose about their limited 'finds'. This will suit the short-visit tourist adequately but walks tend to be basic, without the little diversions that make them exciting. Another model is the *'back-of-my-hand'* local enthusiast who will know every twisty turn, diversion and staggering view in the locality and describe them for you as well as he/she can. This well suits the adventurous walker who wants the best and doesn't mind deciphering opaque explanations and still getting lost. When you know something very well it's easy to assume rather than explain. Some fine guides endeavour to combine both, in a rich compromise.

This guide is certainly not better or worse than those approaches; it's just different. It will suit some readers. The intention is for the reader to explore a fantastic area alongside the author. As I discover, I report so that you can find it, too. You might learn about the Monmouth Hereford border alongside me, but not from me.

And roughly speaking, as a guide, anything in italics can be skipped over – probably the best thing to do.

On litter…

Self-evidently, walkers enjoy and respect the countryside and do not leave litter, so this book does not exhort you to *'take it home'*. However, for myself I go one step further. It is my practice to take 4-pence carrier bag on every walk and set myself the target of filling it with cans, bottles and plastics before the end of the walk. Sadly, this is not a difficult challenge. Patently, one old chap with a carrier bag will not make a dent in our litter problem, but it is good to feel that you left it better than you found it if only slightly. As guests/custodians in an unbelievable landscape perhaps it behoves us to make a positive contribution, be it never so small.

On safety…

Dress for weather that will change in a matter of minutes. Don't run out of light; it goes dark fast! So check the sundown time and allow a big margin for error when planning an outing.

All of these walks have been extensively tested; we find them safe enough – for us. By the time you read it, things can have changed, because of rain, rock falls, erosion or whatever. And your agility might be different from ours, so you must judge the safety of every enterprise you undertake. We are not saying that any walk is safe today or for you, only that it was safe when we did it, for us.

We will not accept responsibility for misfortune that occurs on your walk. You walk at your own risk!

And health…

This walking lark is worth it for the breath-taking views but to make it healthy they recon you need to be a little breathless on the ascents but still able to hold a conversation. *(Mind you that last bit always looks a bit dodgy when I walk alone.)* Carry sun block and lip-balm for regular application, in summer, especially if you're not well thatched. Carry copious water. Sometimes I don't get thirsty at all and the next time, a litre is gone in no time. Possibly we are affected by humidity. When the air is very dry and whipping past on a hot day it does seem to rip the moisture out of you.

Blisters happen, so I carry plasters. I also carry a spare pair of shoes and socks, as different from the ones I am walking in as possible. That means that if a shoe is rubbing I can put on another pair that does not have the same pressure points. Wear sun protecting clothes or sou'westers, as appropriate.

A compass and map will get you home wherever you are and a whistle is good in the event that you want to attract attention. Cell signal is pretty good here, now, so take a 'phone and know where you are should you need to summon aid.

On paths…

I use the term 'path' rather loosely in places. Some are thin but clear, sometimes they vanish without warning. I find that if the path vanishes, it's usually because I've wondered off it. If I stop and look around I usually spot it and return is easy. Sometimes it just peters out. Then it is good to have Hiawatha with you; if you can see trainer prints every now and then you are probably still on the route.

Sometimes you realise that it is not a path at all, but a sheep trail; sometimes a rain gulley.

There are also '*Hogwarts paths*' that can be clear as day from a distance but when you reach them and try to follow them, they will completely vanish. Hereford '*Hogwart's paths*' appear and disappear at will. I personally think that they do so simply to inconvenience walkers.

> Jerome K Jerome says of kettles, 'one must pretend to take no notice of it, if you want it to boil. It is a good plan, too, to talk loudly about how you don't feel like tea and will probably not drink any of it when it's ready, anyway, and would really prefer lemonade.'
>
> I find the same works for some paths. If I say to you 'Pick path A' or 'Take track B' you will not find either in a month of weekends. If we pretend not to care about paths at all, then one will pop up in no time. Just until it thinks you are beginning to like following it and then it will instantly vanish. I tried a good trick on one. When I stumbled upon it I turned and followed it backwards for that way it was as clear as day. The path was happy to be followed as long as it thought it was leading me in the wrong direction. Before long it smelled a rat, though, and realized that I was liking following it so 'Poof!' it was gone.

> *So, like Jerome, we give out that we do not want to use the path anyway. One day we are on a 'path unlooked for' and we follow it for a bit, loudly saying things like, 'I'm not bothered about this path either way. Are you?' 'No not me; I'm happy keeping the stream on my left elbow; don't need a path at all, really. Aren't you the same?' 'Oh, yes, that's good enough for me; I've no use for a path.' Keeping this up means that the path continues for some way before it cottons on to our ruse and then 'Poof!' It is gone.*

Anyway, each walk is independently pilot tested to assure me that the description works, so you'll be OK, and even if you are unable to find a trail (maybe it was washed away) a road always materialises.

On equipment…

A compass and a map make a good start. That way, you'll find a route under any circumstances. More importantly, when you reach a high peak, you're surrounded by views over a range of villages, mountains and whatnot and it is great fun to sit and identify each from the map.

Some people walk in hiking boots, but for most of these walks, in summer waterproof walking trainers are enough. Only where walking is over very rocky ground would a hard sole be advisable to prevent meta-tarsal bruising. The walk guide will warn you. For muddy winter walking, though, wellies are as good as anything.

I take spare footwear, as different from what I have on my feet as possible. If I get a blister, I can change into something with different pressure points. Sandals, in the summer for instance mean that blistered toes are safe.

Water is crucial. Decide how much you need for the number of hours that you will walk and double it. On some occasions, when the wind is strong and the humidity very low, water loss can be quite remarkable. A cold beer is recommended in many of the walks but that's not always the best way to re-hydrate. Take plenty of water before starting on the *Wye Valley, Bitter*.

Take sun cream in the summer for periodic reapplying, and protective headwear *(especially if you are folically challenged)*.

A stick has two benefits.

> Firstly, on some walks the ground is unsteady because gravel and stones can move underfoot. A third point of contact can be a life-saver when the ground slips and your feet go out from under you. My stick has saved me on many occasions.

> Secondly, in terms of exercise value, using a stick is an upper limb workout to complement your lower limb exercise. Alternate hands and you will develop muscle evenly.

> Occasionally, even in summer, you'll bepleased that have lightweight raingear in your backpack. This is Wales; when it rains here it doesn't mess around!

Places to visit

A few of our favourites, but not an exhaustive list:

1. Symonds Yat Rock, Symonds Yat East
    a. See: peregrine falcon nest;
    b. See: the most impressive far reaching views and walk in the forest.
    c. Walk down to Symonds Yat East, through the woods and sit a while by the river, watch the hand ferry, or drop in at the Saracen's Head for some good real ales.

2. Symonds Yat West:
    a. Butterfly Zoo
    b. Amazing Hedge Maze and so many other mazes.
    c. 1-hour riverboat trips on the Wye
    d. Hire a rowing boat by the hour 01600 890 733

3. Canoeing on the Wye. 01600891100 http://www.canoethewye.co.uk
    a. Collect a canoe from Ross-on-Wye or Symonds Yat and they will drive you upstream so that you can canoe back to your car. Find details in the Log Cabin.
    b. ¼-day, ½-day, full-day. You set the time and they take you upstream accordingly.
    c. Try the full 2-day adventure, canoeing from Hay on Wye to Monmouth.

4. Clearwell Cave, near Coleford.
   A natural cave once used as a tin mine (full of fab old machinery!)

5. Castles, including:
    a. Skenfrith – on the Abergavenny Rd. Free; good swimming; lovely village
    b. Goodrich – off the A40, North of Monmouth
    c. White castle – on the Abergavenny road
    d. Grosmont Castle - off the Abergavenny road
    e. Raglan Castle on the A34, West out of Monmouth.

6. Steam railway – Coleford

7. Sculpture Walk or cycle path – Coleford

8. Market towns you'll enjoy and aplenty, but these are a few not ot be missed:

   Ledbury, Tewkesbury, Monmouth, Ross-on-Wye, Old Hereford, Leominster.

9. And to eat or drink start with The Royal Arms, in Llangrove. Our favourite! A very welcoming pub; I have never found such a matey atmosphere anywhere. They're happy to see your dogs (on leads), and children. Even some adults are admitted. Free WiFi (*Tha'ts email, not a swinger's club*). Very popular take away menu.

   Really, there are many good public houses, here and for each walk we'll suggest at least one.

Llancloudy to Llangrove (*and the fabulous Royal Arms*)

This is a 1-hour each-way, walk, moderately strenuous, with fine views. It takes us through fields, woods, a lovely stream and has a quite excellent public house as a half-way reward.

The Royal Arms provides very good inexpensive home cooked food; have very agreeable bar staff and excellent beers and wines.

Take a compass, binoculars, a map and your stick.

Some walks take us over well-trodden paths where your heart-attack will see you discovered and revived in mere minutes. We love this one, though, because it takes us on *the path less Travelled* (Frost,1920) and when you are eventually found it will be no more than your bleached bones that remain to decorate the scenery.

Park in Llancloudy. The campsite will happily allow this if you email p0071028@brookes.ac.uk for permission.

If you enjoy geocaching, find and autograph the book in the geocache box near the campsite entrance.
https://www.geocaching.com/

Leave the campsite, walking uphill passing the Chapel. On the left there is a signed footpath

Follow the hedge, traversing one field, through the gap to the top of the next field and follow the hedge around to your left keeping the hedge on your Right until you see a gate on your Right signed footpath.

From here, look back and you can make out your car in the campsite.

Follow the hedge to a beautiful cottage on your left and ahead you will see a style letting onto a narrow lane.

This one can be slightly difficult for dog walkers as it does not have facilities for dog passage.
Climb over the stile, cross the lane and enter the field by kissing gate signed footpath

hedge, which is well tended or neglected according to the season and depending on how rapidly the weeds are growing.

You will pass through a gate and continue to the crest of the hill where there is another stile, signed footpath. This one can be more difficult as, again, it does not have facilities for dog passage.

Diagonally to your right you will see another stile. This field may be mowed, or may be growing nettles, according to season.
Step over the style or through the metal hunting gate and follow the hedge on your left.
There is a narrow path against the

Cross the next field, diagonally, to your right. It is easiest to aim for the electricity pylon depicted in picture.
This field is often planted with wheat, but there is usually a very clear footpath.

You approach a hedge and will see a gap signed footpath, through which you drop down to a stream.

Using this footpath, you walk down through the trees to a charming bridge over the stream.

7

Once over the stream, climb the steep hill, up and a little left, again guided by that pylon. This field is often planted out with Maize and the well-maintained path can give you the eerie experience of being completely enclosed by impenetrable greenery.

Pass to the right of the Pylon (finally) and you will see a gap in the hedge ahead of you.

Cross the track at this gap and you see a footpath signed ahead of you, following the hedge.

Follow this path through two fields separated by a stile.
Look out for a nice pond on your right.

You come out of the final field, cross a lane, and take the lane immediately ahead of you signed Royal Arms Inn and walk for about 5-mins to enter Llangrove find the fine public house on your Right. Llangrove has a fine church and a range of attractive houses. Most of all there is this excellent Pub *(Did I mention that?)* There is outdoor and indoor seating and if you say you started from the Meredith Farm Campsite you will be well received.

There is a Geocache, here, too, should you feel inclined to apply your Monica, again.

The Royal Arms is one of those bars where it is terribly hard to buy a drink.
(No, not that; the service is excellent!)

You recall when we were young and not so flush:
"Your round, I reckon Tom." "No. Can't be. I got one in last Thursday" No you didn't, you tight fisted git. That was the week before; come on, anti up!" "OK, but I think you're taking advantage of my good nature." "You don't have one; get your hand in your pocket." etc, etc.

Now it is:
"I'll get that."
"Hold your horses, Tom. John has said he's buying this one and Chris has been waiting since yesterday. And Martin's ahead of you, too.
Anyway, you've got two in as it is!"

8

Coppett Hill

This is a 3-hour walk, moderately strenuous, with fine views. It takes us through fields, woods, a grand river and has a quite excellent public house as a terminal reward.
A fine walk, but muddy in winter. Great for dogs!

Take your stick!
Some walks take us over well-trodden paths where your heart-attack will see you discovered and revived in mere minutes. We love this one, though, because it takes us on the path less Travelled (Frost,1920) and when you are eventually found it will be no more than your bleached bones that remain to decorate the scenery.

Drive into Goodrich Village, off the A40, North of Monmouth and take the road on your Right signed Welsh Bicknor. Cross a charming old road bridge and reach a small village triangle. Pass to the Left of this, pass three houses, the last being The Quarry House and look for a small old quarry on your right, in which it is convenient to park.

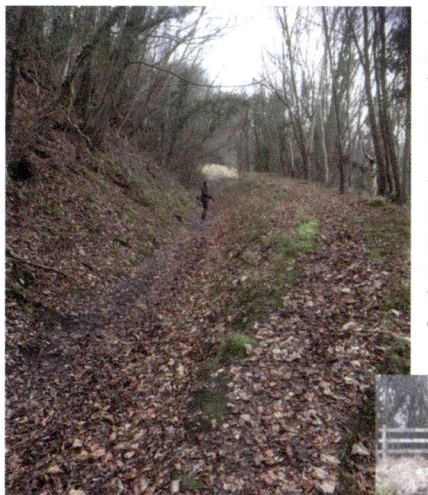

Take the signed footpath up from the quarry up into the woods. This is a fine walk through ancient trees following a stone wall behind which lies a dramatic inland cliff.

The path forks; you will want the Left fork, in the end, but first, walk a short distance on the right-hand path and you will see a nicely restored lime kiln and from this vantage enjoy a rather splendid view down over the valley.

Retrace your steps, and take the other path, which takes you over the top of the lime kiln.

9

The path is good when it has been maintained, although after wind or snow you might have to clamber around or over fallen timber.

Continue up through the woods, marvelling at the wall on the Left, which does no more than wall of the inland cliff.
Labour was cheap once.

(Oh yes, also marvel at the inland cliff itself. The whole of the Wye valley is lined with these magnificent features.)
Continue up the path and you will find steps. Look closely and you will see that you are climbing through an old hill fort. There are a great many hill forts to be seen, locally, with the best imaginable position being at Symonds Yat East. (Tomorrow's walk.)

You emerge from the trees at a Trigonometric (Trig) point, where the views are pretty impressive. However if you walk uphill for a further hundred yards you will find the ruins of a folly and from there the views are even better.

Take time to identify: Goodrich Castle, Ross on Wye, the A40, Goodrich Village, Symonds Yat, the winding River Wye, etc. They can all be seen from where you are standing.

You continue up and over the hill, passing four ancient spring-fed ponds created for watering stock and now being carefully preserved.
Keeping the wall to your left takes you down on a clear path through splendid woodlands to open onto a field and you can then walk to the river Wye.

Here you will be almost at the foot of the huge inland cliff under the Symonds Yat viewing point. Look up and you can just see people looking down. That'll be us, next weekend!   We turn Right and follow the river across this flood plain field waving to the canoeists and eventually pass through a metal gate onto a stone track, leading towards a farmhouse. After a second gate and before reaching the house, you will see a signposted footpath on your right leading up into the woods.

Follow this path uphill and it will bring you out at a charming collection of cottages, with a byway/road that takes you back to our 3-way junction at Welsh Bicknor – the triangle that you drove past earlier.

As you recognise this place you could return by road to the quarry. However, it is more fun to take the signed footpath on the Right up the hill past brilliant rocks, back to the trig point. (picture)

From here it is a fine walk back down over the limekiln to your car.

*Having been led so disastrously astray by this enthusiastic guide you will wonder **why do I do it?** ...and I am quite unable to give you a good answer. There is no reasonable excuse. However, it might make you feel better if you were to pop into 'The Hostelarie' in Goodrich,*

or our old favourite, the Royal Arms, in Llangrove; you know, a good real ale really does make you feel better.

Coppett Hill, shorter alternative

This is a 2-hour walk, moderately strenuous, with very fine views. It takes us through fields and woods, and has a quite excellent public house as a terminal reward.
Muddy in the winter; good for dogs.

Take your stick.

Some walks take us over well-trodden paths where your heart-attack will see you discovered and revived in mere minutes. We love this one, though, because it takes us on *the path less Travelled* (Frost,1920) and when you are eventually found it will be no more than your bleached bones that remain to decorate the scenery.

Drive to Goodrich Village and take the road signed Welsh Bicknor. Cross a charming old road bridge and reach a village small triangle. Pass to the Left of this, pass three houses, the last being The Quarry House and look for a small old quarry on your right, in which it is convenient to park.

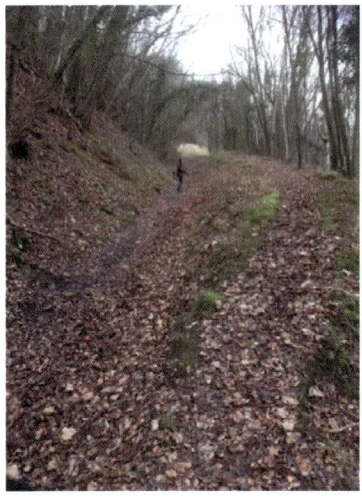

Take the signed footpath up from the quarry up into the woods. This is a fine walk through ancient trees following a stone wall behind which lies a dramatic inland cliff.

The path forks. You will want the Left fork, in the end, but first, walk a short distance on the right path and you will see a nicely restored lime kiln and from this vantage enjoy a rather splendid view down over the valley.
Retrace your steps, and take the other path, which takes you right over the top of the lime kiln.

The path is good when it has been maintained, but after wind or snow you might have to clamber around or over fallen timber.

Continue up through the woods, marvelling at the wall on the left, which does no more than wall of the inland cliff.
Labour was cheap once.

(Oh yes, also marvel at the inland cliff itself. The whole of the Wye valley is lined with these magnificent features.)

Continue up the path and you will find steps. Look closely and you will see that you are climbing through an old hill fort. There are a great many hill forts to be seen, locally, with the best imaginable position being at Symonds Yat.

You emerge from the trees at a Trigonometric (Trig) point, where the views are pretty impressive. However if you walk uphill for a hundred yards you find the ruins of a folly and from there the views are even better.

Take time to identify: Goodrich Castle, Ross on Wye, the A40, Goodrich Village, Symonds Yat, the winding River Wye, etc.

They can all be seen from where you are standing.

You continue up and over the hill, passing three ponds created for watering stock and Facing away from the Folly, you can see paths downhill, through the bracken.

Follow one of these and it will bring you out at a charming collection of cottages, with a byway/road that takes you into a three-way junction in Welsh Bicknor.

You will recognise this road and could return by the road to the quarry. However, if you have a little energy left, it is better to take the signed footpath on the Right up the hill past brilliant rocks, to the trig point. From here it is a fine walk back down over the limekiln to your car.

Having been led astray by this enthusiastic walking guide you will now be wondering, 'Why do you do it?', and I am quite unable to answer you. There is no reasonable excuse. It might make you feel better if you were to pop into the fine public house, 'The Hostelarie' in Goodrich, or drive a few minutes to reach our personal favourite, the Royal Arms, in Llangrove where a good real ale does do something to make you feel a little better.

Over your beer, though, do congratulate yourself that you took the shorter option.

The important thing is to swear that never again will you undertake a Wheeler Walk.

Garway Hill

This is a 2-hour walk, moderately strenuous, with fine views. It takes us over a fine, ancient common, wqith views over several counties has a quite excellent public house as a terminal reward.
Muddy in the winter; good for dogs.

Take your stick, a compass and a map.

Some walks take us over well-trodden paths where your heart-attack will see you discovered and revived in mere minutes. This is one such, although we really like those that take us on *the path less Travelled* (Frost,1920) and when you are eventually found it will be no more than your bleached bones that remain to decorate the scenery.

Drive up the B4521, Abergavenny to Broad Oak Road. *(Broad Oak is the location of the world's best garage).*

From Broad Oak, take the Garway Road, passing the quite splendid Garway Moon Inn, on Garway Common. (*Remember this. You'll want it later!*)

Drive through Garway, a pleasant village worth a few minutes, and turn Right following signposts to Garway Hill.

Continue until you see a Public House with an old Rising Sun), on a track on house (a former inn sign The the Left.

This is an unpromising looking road, but quite passable and there is good parking at the top. From there you step through a gate, with footpath sign onto Garway Hill Common Land.

Turn a little to the right and follow the path uphill. You will see a trig point and a building on the apex of the hill, which is an old wartime RAF look-out.
Walking towards that point, you will see a large and very fine pond on your right,

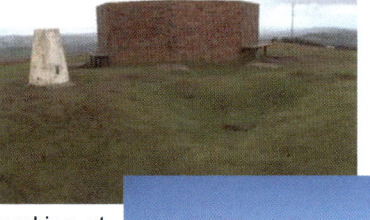

involving considerable earthworks and needing a little of your time for exploration.

Reaching the vantage point of the Trigonometric (Trig) Point you can see for miles.

Using map and compass you can locate the black mountains in one direction, Simmonds Yat in another and if you are careful you can see the square tower of St Weonards Church that is visible from all over the area. There are many other hamlets and villages to be seen and it is pleasing to use the map to give a name to each. You can also see Ross-on-Wye, May Hill, Skirrid Fawr, Sugarloaf Mountain and the Forest of Dean
Herefordshire is called the least populated county in the UK and standing at this point it is easy to see how that might be true.

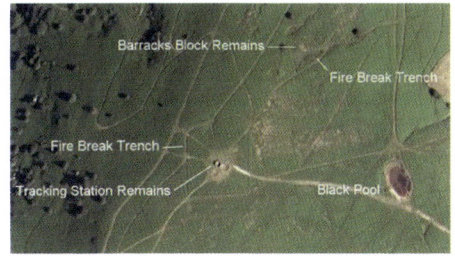

The old RAF building is still good and worth studying. It used to have a wooden top giving considerable additional height but now just the stonework remains. There is also the remains of a barracks over to the right as we approach the tower.

This is a favourite point for flying model airplanes.
From here you can see the network of paths available to you and you can plan a meander back to the car that will be as long or short as you want.
We recommend heading away in on the path downwards from the Trig point slowly circling around to the left, through some very attractive common land with stunted trees and bracken to gently return to the parking area. Notice trenches as fire breaks to control bracken fires.

*Now, once again, you have been led astray by an enthusiastic walking guide and once again you are wondering, **'Why do I do it?'***
Once again, I am quite unable to answer you. There is no reasonable excuse, although it might make you feel better if you were to pop into the fine public house, we noted earlier, The Garway Moon. It's a fine place for post-perambulatory ale. They have a keen kitchen, too.
Actually, this might be a good time to repent; let's swear that this time we really will be strong and refuse to take any more of these crazy walks. Maybe we should sign the pledge, now…

15

I, the undersigned,

(insert name here)

In the company of all of those present, do hereby pledge, assert and promise that nevermore and without exception or exemption will I be persuaded, cajoled, bribed or coerced into undertaking another crazy and disastrous Wheeler Walk.

I will withstand threats, intimidations and inducements and hold resolute to this oath right up until that day when my resolve fails.

(Sign here)

Witnesses:

(All those present sign here)

Symonds Yat

This is a 1/2-hour walk, moderately strenuous, with fine views and through lovely woods, down to a splendid river. It has a quite excellent public house as a ½-way reward.
Muddy in the winter; good for dogs.

Take your stick!

Some walks take us over well-trodden paths where your heart-attack will see you discovered and revived in mere minutes. This is one such, although we really prefer those that take us on *the path less Travelled* (Frost,1920) and when you are eventually found it will be no more than your bleached bones that remain to decorate the scenery.

From the A40 at Whitchurch, just East of Monmouth, we take the turning signed Symonds Yat East.
We do not drive to Symonds Yat East village, itself, but rather follow signs uphill to the Symonds Yat Rock (viewing point), where there is easy access and ample paid parking.
There is good Tea, Coffee & Cake, to be had in a log-cabin here, but perhaps you'd prefer to wait until you reach the Saracen's Head Inn, at the midpoint of your walk. Maybe both.

Before starting, walk uphill past the café, noticing that you are passing through one of the county's many hill forts, and continue over a foot bridge crossing the road to The Rock. This is at the head of a huge inland cliff overlooking the River Wye on three sides.

This is the cliff which we saw from river level when on the Coppett Hill walk, last week.
Surely, if we squint in a special way, we can see ourselves standing in the flood plain staring up in a puzzled sort of way at us now. Time, after all, is an illusion brought about by the passage of history {Adams,1978; Einstein,1952}

This piece of land can be imagined as the finest of prehistoric defensive points no surprise that we have just passed through a hill fort, earthworks.

17

From here we look across at a number of other inland cliffs and nesting in one there has been a pair of peregrine falcons, successfully breeding for the past several years. There is usually a guard mounted here by the RSPB and they are always pleased to let you use their telescope to look closely at these birds.

In truth, you could walk as much as you want in any direction from here, but we are recommending a steep but manageable walk down through the woods to Symonds Yat East which is a delightful village on the Wye.

We return towards the log cabin and see a signposted path on the right down into the woods, passing a small cave on our right.
Down and down, we go, crossing over a small green lane, until we emerge at the quite lovely River.

Here, notice Japanese Knot Weed on the river bank and be amazed by the fabulous position of houses all the way up the valley side opposite you, over the river.

Admire the design of and maybe try the hand ferry. This has a high overhead cable for propelling the boat without obstructing the passage of river boats beneath, although it is no distance downstream to the rapids, so this is still a turning point for most cruise boats.

btw, If you fancy a boat trip, then one can be boarded by driving, later, to Symonds Yat West. Or hire a boat by calling 01600 890 733.

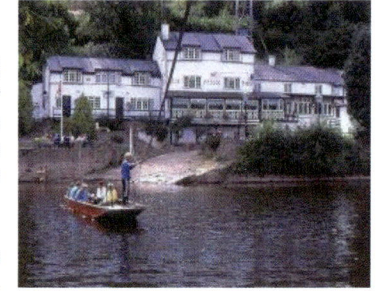

Take tea in the lovely, if unfortunately named, Rose Cottage Tea room, or a beer in the Saracen's Head Inn.

There is always a good range of Wye Valley Brewery ales to be had, fine wines and good food. This is a very busy place at weekends, but well managed, so it is always possible to get served.

From here, you can all walk back up through the woods to the car park, or maybe just send the driver to fetch the car and drive back to you while you enjoy another beer.

The Three Castles Walk

Grosmont Castle was an occupied aristocratic residence; Skenfrith and White Castles were garrisons and defensive points. Therefore the soldiery had to move quickly between the three interconnected castles and thus was the route established. The walk persists and is popular as a badge of achievement if completed as a one-day outing. This is entirely doable but does entail very hard and non-stop effort and leaves little time to enjoy the walk and the fabulous scenery involved. We prefer to see it as two, or better still three, good walks so that we can also enjoy the amazing countryside and the rather good public houses on the route.

Take two cars. Park one car at one castle; drive everyone to the second castle and walk back to the first car.
(Be careful to manage the keys carefully. To arrive and car 2 and realise that the necessary car keys are safely in the pocket of car 1 is not a good formula.)
Each section of the walk takes you up high hills, through woodland and over streams. Each is as picturesque as the others.

The 3-Castles: Step one: White castle to Grosmont Castle.

This is a 3-hour walk, quite strenuous, with fine views and through lovely woods, down to the splendid village of Grosmont, where, thankfully, there is a splendid Public House, currently in the collective ownership of the village (A community Pub). Muddy in the winter; good for dogs.

Take your stick!

Some walks take us over well-trodden paths where your heart-attack will see you discovered and revived in mere minutes. This is none such, however. This takes us on *the path less Travelled* (Frost,1920) and when you are eventually found it will be no more than your bleached bones that remain to decorate the scenery.

Drive to Grosmont and park car No 1. In car 2, drive the whole party to White Castle which can be found signposted from the B4521 road from Abergavenny to Broad Oak.

Walk back to White Castle Cottage, turn left and return to the B4521. Turn right and follow the road for about 200m. This little stretch of busy highway is about all of the roadwork that we do until nearing Grosmont.

19

In front of a cottage on the left of the road, turn to the left onto a sunken path that slowly rises. This is the beginning of some serious climbing to be undertaken today!

At the top of the path, turn right on to an unclassified road and follow this around to the right, passing Lower Green and Upper Green, until you come to a turning on your left signed to Saint Mary's Church. Follow this cul-de-sac until you see the graveyard on your left. Go through the gate and cross to the gate on the other side. Follow the waymark to the right and cross the field towards a small wooded area with a pond. Cross the next stile and the field, keeping the small brick building on your right and the stand of oak trees to your left until you reach the next stile.

Cross the field diagonally left towards the line of trees, keeping the summit of the hill on your right. The next stile is at the end of the fence line on your left. At this stile cross diagonally left towards the tree line.

You reach and ford Pont Brook and turn right over the next stile, go through an orchard and follow the waymarks to the road, keeping the tree line and stream to your right. Crossing the road stile, turn left and follow the road. At the next junction turn right and follow the road to a field gate.

Follow the path up the hill to the farthest tree line, bearing slightly left at the stile in the middle of the field. Follow the path through the woods to reach a forestry commission track.

The area has some of the largest sustainable timber forests in the country, a great deal of which passes through the timber yard at Pontrialis.

Turn left and follow the track through the woods. Keep following this track until you come to a stile on your left leading into a field. Cross this and go downhill, keeping the tree line to your right. Here, two footpaths cross. Go over the stile and bear to the right, following a rough, muddy farm track downhill.

20

After passing through Barns Farm, go through the gate and follow the road down to Tresenny Brook. Cross the stream over the footbridge and follow the path up to Grosmont and its castle.

The Angel Inn (Community pub) will now offer you splendid post-perambulatory beer and hear how you got on with the walk.

Here we can be thankful that the day's pain is finished, but is there another two days to come?

Are we mad? Yes, probably.

Maybe, next time you can bring an excuse and get out of walking.

Perhaps a note from your Mother would help?

Major Winging RA (ret)
Welldoneroaming
Wimp's bottom
Sloth, Berks
ID11 5OD

Dear Dr Wheeler,

Please excuse Neil from strenuous and unnatural walking on account of his having Wimpout Syndrome. Sadly he seems to have an acute exacerbation of the condition since he bought your fine book.

Yours,

Maj Arthur Winging (Mrs)

The 3-Castles: Step Two: Grosmont Castle to Skenfrith Castle.

This is another 3-hour section, quite strenuous, with fine views and through lovely woods, down to a delightful river and then on to the splendid village of Skenfrith, where, thankfully, there is another splendid Public House, (with a dog&boot bar). Muddy in the winter; good for dogs. Very little road-work. *(The walk; not the bar)*

Take your stick!
Some walks take us over well-trodden paths where your heart-attack will see you discovered and revived in mere minutes. This is none such, however. This takes us on *the path less Travelled* (Frost,1920) and when you are eventually found it will be no more than your bleached bones that remain to decorate the scenery.

Drive to Skenfrith on the B4521, between Abergavenny and Ross, and park car no 1. In car no 2m drive the whole party to Grosmont and park.

Grosmont Castle is a major feature of the village and was the birthplace of Henry, 1st Duke of Lancaster. Grosmont originated as an Iron Age camp and grew into a medieval market town, granted a borough charter in 1219, and by 1250 boasted 160 dwellings. It had a mayor and (more importantly) an official ale taster!

From the castle, at the main road turn left (South) down towards Lower Tresenny. Cross Tresenny Brook again and follow the road round to the left until you come to a stile on your right. Cross this stile and follow the path uphill to another stile and cross, now keeping the fence to your right. When you get to a farm gate, cross the stile and follow the edge of the field with the hedge on your left.

Cross a footbridge, then follow the left side of the field towards Little Cross. Follow the path behind the barn. Cross the stile to your right in front of the farmhouse and head directly uphill. After crossing three fields, cross the stile and bear left towards the evergreen tree line.

Enter the woods, following a sunken path that continues uphill. After a steep climb through the woods, the path comes to a stile leading to an open field. Cross this stile and follow the fence to the other side of the field. the other side of the field, cross the stile and bear left across the field towards some derelict farm buildings.

Follow the waymark post to the right of these ruins and then a track that zigzags around a barn. At the bottom of this track turn left, following the waymark. Cross the stile and keeping the fence on your right, and cross a further two fields. In the right-hand corner of the second field, cross a stile to the left of a gate. Follow the track to a fence, and bear right down to a stile.

Cross the stile and follow the waymarks downhill. At a fence by a wood, turn right then left at the end of the fence. Go over the stile on to a single-track road. Follow this down to the Grosmont road and turn right. Stay on the road until you see a track on your Left for Box Farm. Turn left, then follow the track through the Farm. At the farm turn left through the farm buildings. Go through the gate and follow the track towards Trevonny.

At the third gate, turn right towards a stile next to a large tree. Cross the stile and follow the fence on your left. Keeping the farm on your left, follow the track down to a gate. Cross the stile and a field to the next gate. Cross the next stile and follow the hedge on your left. Cross the next stile. At this point you should see the river Monnow down on your left. At this point, keep to the right of the fence and follow it across to the other side of the field.

23

Incidentally, thank you for buying this book of walks, but...

> *... for goodness sake, whatever you do: Don't walk the walk. (Just talk the talk like everyone else does.) These walks take you to sights beyond anything you could ever hope to see; where no human eye has ever set foot, most likely.*
>
> *Look at me. I've always loved the countryside, but this is addiction. I get out there, away from it all and marvel at a unique and unreal landscape every chance I get. I used to be a jolly, chubby, rotund, sedate sort of gent with umbrella and bowler hat, breathless just looking at a flight of stairs, but now all of that has gone. I've lost stones; my fat has turned to grizzly old leg muscle and I walk up mountains without complaining. I don't want that to happen to you!*
>
> *Running – that's awful; you can see good, honest distress on the faces of runners. It is just a torture invented to inflict pain on fat people. Runners say it's great when they reach the finish line, but that's like banging your head against the wall – it's nice when you stop.*
>
> *But walking is deceptive. It's really fun to be striving to pick out a route to the top of the mountain, or to follow a map, or to decipher the ravings of a walking guide author. The work is hard but you don't notice because the waterfall is exciting or the path enthralling and then suddenly you reach the peak and admire the view of the whole world. (OK, about half of the county really, but to me it's the same thing.) It's still great to sit in the Royal Arms with beer so wholesome and say how glad we are that it's all over, but we never really experienced the pain in the first place. We take pleasure when we stop banging our head, but we never really noticed the pain when we were doing it. No, don't do it. You'll exercise mightily without noticing the discomfort and have such a fab time that you'll never be able to give it up. So much better to never start than to have to kick the habit later.*

Anyway, at the edge of the field, cross the stream and follow the walkway to a stile. Cross this stile and go over another walkway. Follow the waymark posts to a gate and follow a track uphill.

Cross a stile at the top of the hill and pass a house on your right with a pond on your left. After passing the pond, cross a stile and bear right over another on to a track. This track leads down to Skenfrith village, turning left at the bottom towards the church and castle.

Both church and castle need time to explore. The church has an unusual wooden tower.

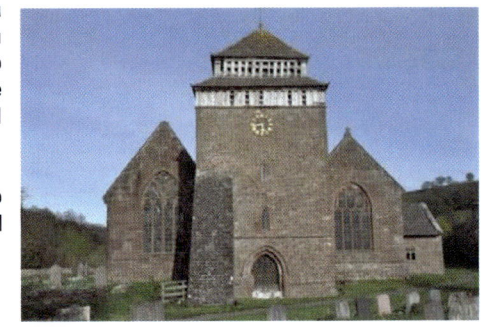

The castle is unmanned, and in good condition, running down to the river where watercourses and sluices remain which once fed the waterwheel, still in place on the back of the water mill.

A twelfth century fortress forming part of the Castles of the Trilateral in the Monnow Valley, Skenfrith Castle was the venue for Dr Who episode Amy's Choice.

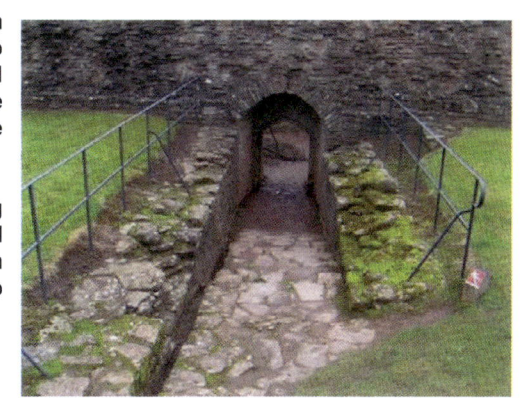

From here it is a very short walk to post-perambulatory ales at the dog&boot bar of the Bell Inn on the bridge. There is every chance that the proprietor will be interested in your exertions, walking between castles, but don't expect sympathy; you really did bring this upon yourself.

The 3-Castles: Step Three: Skenfrith Castle to White Castle.

This is another 3-hour section, quite strenuous, with fine views and through lovely woods, to the splendid White Castle, where, sadly, there is no Public House, but no distance back to The Bell with its dog&boot bar. Muddy in the winter; good for dogs. Very little road-work.

Take your stick!

Some walks take us over well-trodden paths where your heart-attack will see you discovered and revived in mere minutes. This is none such, however. This takes us on *the path less Travelled* (Frost,1920) and when you are eventually found it will be no more than your bleached bones that remain to decorate the scenery.

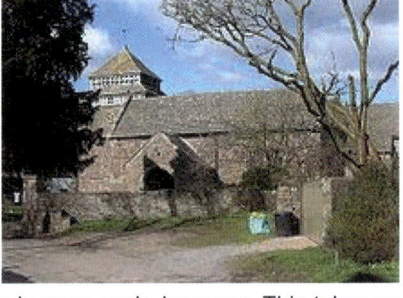

Park car #1 in the carpark of the White castle and drive the entire party in car # 2 to park at Skenfrith Castle.

From the castle, go to the main road and turn right, passing the Bell Inn which will be important to you later. Follow the road for approximately 1.5km. After passing a fine converted schoolhouse on a road junction, from where you can see the Three Castles Campsite, a path is waymarked leaving this main road on the left. Follow the path uphill, keeping the fence or hedge on your left. Go through Lade Farm and follow the track to the road.

Turn right and follow the road as far as a travellers' seat. Follow a track down past Lettravane Farm and past two cottages. The path then narrows and becomes rutted and stony, leading downhill.

At the bottom of this track cross the stile keeping to the right of the derelict barn. Follow the tree line (on your right) downhill to a stream. The building on your left is an old coaching inn. Cross the stile, then the footbridge over the stream. Cross another stile and walk across the field to the opposite fence. Follow this field uphill keeping the fence on your left.

How did this all start?

You know, we only undertook this walk, years ago, because we were all feeling a bit seedy. One of us had a bad knee and giddiness so that he hardly knew what he was doing. The next also had giddiness and hardly knew what she was doing, either. With me, it was liver. I knew it was liver because I had been reading the symptoms on a patent medicine packet and I found that I had them all. It is an extraordinary thing that I have never yet seen a patent medicine advertisement without realizing that I have all of the symptoms described. I think they must target these advertisements terribly well.

I did wonder if it was just clever advertising; but, No. When I looked in a medicine book of the highest repute, I found that indeed it is true; I do have all of those diseases and a good many more besides. It can seem a bit dispiriting to have so many life-threatening problems but if you are careful then the thoroughness of your investigation takes over and your imminent demise from innumerable causes seems to get lost in the exciting study of it all. I found that the Diphtheria was going to be one cause of my eventual failure, but that the yellow fever although classic in its symptomology was in such a mild form that I could survive it for many years if properly controlled.

Anyway, we all thought that exercise and fresh air would be just the thing, so we soon found ourselves struggling up the mountain and down to the river. I'm pretty much cured, but I do find that the others are a bit giddy yet and I'm quite of the view that they rarely know where they are. (With apologies to Gerome)

Anyway, at the next stile, cross and walk towards the farm buildings. Cross a stile, turning right past a small corrugated barn on your right. Follow the farm track for about 50m and cross the next stile on your left. Cross the field, keeping the farm buildings on your left, to the fence or hedge line. Follow this downhill to a stile. Cross this stile and walk downhill to the opposite hedge line. Follow the hedge or fence slightly downhill and cross a stile next to a gate. Walk downhill, keeping the stream and tree line to your left. At the corner of the field, follow the track into the woods.

Cross the stream via the footbridge and bear left to another stile crossing, then bear right and follow the tree line on your right uphill. At the top of the hill, cross a stile over a small field to another stile. Turn right over this stile and follow a track between the woods over a stream. At the end of the track cross the stile and follow the road past Tump Farm.

Follow the road past the barn and the stile next to it. Cross the next stile on your left and follow the hedge on your left. At the tree line, head towards a bridge on the opposite side of the field. Cross the bridge and bear left towards the corner of the field. Follow the edge of the fields, towards a white house, to the road. Turn right and follow the road past Middle Cwm Farm.

About 200-yd past the farm, turn left over a stile and cross the stile in the fence to your right. Follow the fence downhill, bearing slightly right cross a stream at the bottom of the hill. Walk uphill keeping the fence on your left. Cross the next stile on your left and follow the waymark arrow across the field, keeping the large tree in the middle of the field on your left. Cross the next stile and follow the waymark post across the field. Cross the footbridge and turn left. Cross another footbridge and a stile. Walk uphill, keeping the fence on your left. Cross several stiles and fields until you reach the road. Turn right on to the road and follow it back to White Castle.

Here, there is no public House, so we must enjoy the fine castle and then lose no time in returning to The Bell inn and its Dog&boot bar for our usual post perambulatory commiseratory real ale.

Llanthony Priory

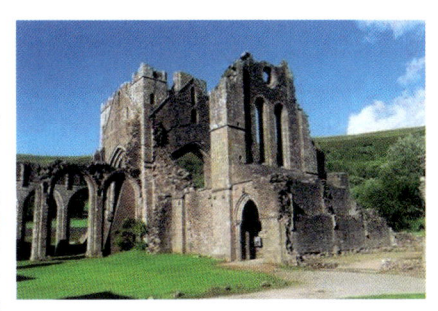

This is a 3-hour walk, quite strenuous, with fine views and through lovely woods. Take your stick!

Some walks take us over well-trodden paths where your heart-attack will see you discovered and revived in mere minutes. This is none such, however. Parts of this walk take us on *the path less Travelled* (Frost,1920) and when you are eventually found it will be no more than your bleached bones that remain to decorate the scenery. We take a low-level route to Llanthony Abbey but return by higher paths on wilder terrain using Open Access land.

There is a fine public house, the Half Moon at out ½-way point.

The road from Pandy (on the A465 Hereford to Abergavenny road) through Llanthony and the Gospel Pass is just about as scenic as any road anywhere. You pass into and out of ancient woodland to cross a cattle grid and suddenly find yourself in moorland, before reaching the mountain pass. From there a climb up a mountain is a must and then it is good to take a Left towards three cocks and Talgarth. This road takes you over still more fabulous open countryside.

This walk covers a short part of that journey by creating a lovely circular route taking in Capel Y Ffin and the largely ruined Llanthony Priory

Drive along the A465 to Pandy and take the lovely road signed Llanthony passing the road to the Priory on out right and continue to park at Capel Y Ffin.

We set out on the main road briefly north but take the first track on the right leading us back down to Blaenau. We continue on a footpath crossing fields to reach a lane.
We continue south-east along the lane towards the Vision Farm and thence on tracks and lanes below the Farm, passing Garn Farm to reach Trevelog.

After 300-yds the lane bends to the right, but we fork left onto a track continuing south.

After a further 300-yds we take the public footpath on the left along the access driveway to Llwyn-on. From here we follow paths across fields past Broadley and reach a lane.

We turn left along the lane and at the first junction, and on striking the main road we turn Left towards the Priory. When the road bends right, we take the footpath on the left across a field to reach Llanthony Priory.
We also pass the Half Moon Inn, so good manners dictate that we partake of a little refreshment!

Returning from the ruined Priory we retrace our route along the exit road. When the access road bears left, we continue straight ahead along the path we used earlier. We pass through a gate and across a field to return to the main road, where we head North.

We fork left at the lane junction, keeping to the main road, and walk up this lane turning left onto an enclosed path following a watercourse. We continue uphill to reach the boundary of Open Access Land., Where we turn right along the flank of Bal Mawr.
The route uses a mixture of paths and tracks above Nantygwyddel Farm as far as Nant-y-Carnau.

From here we regain Open Access Land, passing above Sychtre and then continue along paths, mainly in Open Access Land, for two miles to reach a bridleway. Turn right down the bridleway and descend to a lane. Turn right down the lane to a road junction at Capel-y-ffin and hastily return to the welcome sanctuary of the car. Never has a motor vehicle looked a more welcome site!

A two-minute drive returns us to the Half Moon, where post-peripatetic ale might be forthcoming as well as commiserations from the landlord, when we tell him what we've done.

30

Troubles

At the splendid Half Moon Inn, we like to compete about just how bad we find all of this walking lark; it is so much harder for some of us than it is for others,

> *'Well of course walking for me is particularly difficult because one of my legs is shorter than the other'.*
>
> *'One leg shorter than the other? That's nothing! One of mine is longer than the other and everyone knows that's much worse.'*
>
> *Ha! A couple of mismatched legs is nothing; I've been walking for years with two arthritic hip joints'.*
>
> *Only two arthritic joints? Luxury! I've had Arthritis, Rheumatism and Gout in every joint of my body for ninety-years and a broken ankle for the last ½-mile'.*
>
> *'Arthritis, Rheumatism and Gout in every joint for ninety-years and a broken ankle. I long for such minor problems; you lot don't know what trouble is. I was born with no joints in my legs at all and had to ……..'*

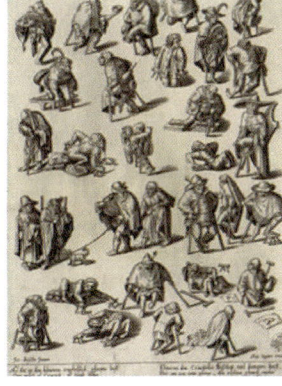

The Sugarloaf Mountain, from Abergavenny; shortest route.

This is a 1½-hour, each-way, walk, moderately strenuous, with fine views. It takes us through open moorland with bracken and woodland. The least painful ascent to a magnificent view.

Take a compass, binoculars, a map and your stick.

Some walks take us over well-trodden paths where your heart-attack will see you discovered and revived in mere minutes. This is the latter, unlike some, we know, that take us on *the path less Travelled* (Frost,1920) such that if you were eventually found it will be no more than your bleached bones that remain to decorate the scenery.

We take the A40 a few miles west from Abergavenny and turn Right into Pentre Road. The road sign is on the Left turning, but we take the right, noticing the Sugarloaf vineyard sign. We take the first turning on our Left and reaching a T-junction turn Left onto Pentre Lane.

The road travels up and North, through a farm and past another where it swings to the Left and following this road eventually leads us to a parking/viewing area.

From here, we take the clear path from the northern side of the parking area, to the Right of the road, heading north-west. The footpath takes us north-west eschewing side paths downhill until we take a wide sweep around to the Right, Eastwads, to the summit of the mountain.

The summit is really a ridge with a steep drop to the north deserving a little caution.

Here we need to spend a good amount of time with Map&Compas, identifying a vast array of features over the 360-deg panorama. We can see across to and beyond the River Usk to our south and well into the Brecon Beacons to our northwest and black mountains, including Skirrid Fawr and Hatterall Hill. On a clear day you can see the Severn Estuary and on into South West England. So, the location requires some time! A thermos and sandwiches may even be called for.

The easiest route back is to retrace our tracks. The return journey always seems so much quicker than the outward and this one, being downhill all of the way is no exception.

This was a shorter walk than it might have been, although a bit steep, so over a post-perambulatory real ale we are able to congratulate ourselves that at least we didn't fall for Wheeler's blarney and walk the long route.

Now, the nearest traditional pub is the Lamb and Flag back on the A40. We consider that this is an essential next step, and the pub-food is not to be passed up, either. It's no real compensation for the pain we've just experienced, but, well, at least it's all over. And we did take the shorter route.

The Sugarloaf Mountain, from Abergavenny, longer, circular route.

This is a 3-hour, circular, walk, moderately strenuous, with fine views. It takes us through open moorland with heather and woodland. A descent walk and a magnificent view.

Take a compass, binoculars, a map and your stick.

Some walks take us over well-trodden paths where your heart-attack will see you discovered and revived in mere minutes. this is one such, unlike some, we know, that take us on *the path less Travelled* (Frost,1920) such that if you were eventually found it will be no more than your bleached bones that remain to decorate the scenery.

There's a good pub to look forward to

We take the A40 a few miles west from Abergavenny and turn Right into Pentre Road. The road sign is on the Left turning, but we take the right, noticing the Sugarloaf vineyard sign. We take the first turning on our Left and reaching a T-junction turn Left onto Pentre Lane.

The road travels up and North, through a farm and past another where it swings to the Left and following this road eventually leads us to a parking/viewing area.

From the car park we walk a short distance back down the road and head up onto the grass on the left-hand side. We continue along this straight and wide grass path climbing above the road until reaching the woodland edge. The woods have some beach as well as these stunted but ancient oaks. There are occasional larger specimens. The woods were used for charcoal production as were many woodlands hereabouts and throughout the Forest of Dean. Various signs of this activity can still be seen.

We walk down into the ancient, predominantly oak woodland, travelling north in the direction of the summit, running gently down the other side of the ridge from the grassy path which we just traversed. We continue through this splendid wood until we reach the head of a stream junction.

We continue to follow the path, running straight up the stream valley to the north-east. There is nothing for it but to puff-and-grunt our way to the ridge, thinking all of the way how this must be doing us *'the power of good'*. Pausing occasionally, pretending it is to appreciate the view, we can see Abergavenny and the Usk Valley.

The summit is a ridge with a steep drop to the north deserving a little caution.

Here we need to spend a good amount of time with Map&Compas, identifying a vast array of features over the 360-deg panorama. We can see across to and beyond the River Usk to our south and well into the Brecon Beacons to our northwest and black mountains, including Skirrid Fawr and Hatterall Hill. On a clear day you can see the Severn Estuary and on into South West England. Mind you this is Wales; we don't have that many really clear days!

From the Sugarloaf summit at certain times of the year we will see endless, beautiful purple heather. Patches and strips are cut to break up the even-aged heather, and fire is used create a wider range of habitats for wildlife. The new growth, offers far more food value for birds and small mammals than the older woody material, so the heather is managed to maximise the wildlife benefit.

Facing the side of the trig point which shows National Trust sign we begin our descent by the path in front and to our right. The path drops diagonally down, with the summit to our right, reaching a grass path running alongside a ditch and bank. This is likely to be an ancient (early medieval) boundary. Labour was cheap!

We follow the path alongside the bank and continue down the path on the ridge. Eventually we see a fence on our right. Walk along the track roughly parallel to this fence, until the fence turns a corner down the hill. From here the path returns us downhill and we can see the blessed sanctuary of our car, which we so unwisely left a few hours ago.

This has been a longer walk and a bit steep, so post-perambulatory real ales are essential and the nearest traditional pub is the Lamb and Flag back on the A40.

We consider that this is an essential next step, and the pub-food is not to be passed up, either.

It's no real compensation for the pain we've just experienced, but, well, at least it's all over.

Mind you, if we had to look at that incredible view (and we did have to) then there was a shorter option, you know!

36

Little Skirrid Mountain from Abergavenny circuit.

This is a 2-hour, circular, walk, moderately strenuous, with fine views. It takes us through woodland onto a clear peak having a magnificent view.

Take a compass, binoculars, a map and your stick.

Some walks take us over well-trodden paths where your heart-attack will see you discovered and revived in mere minutes. this is one such, unlike some, we know, that take us on *the path less Travelled* (Frost,1920) such that if you were eventually found it will be no more than your bleached bones that remain to decorate the scenery.

Take the A465 from Abergavenny towards Hereford and turn Right onto the B4521 from Towards Skenfrith (A fine village with many walks and a fine boot&dog bar) and on the Left-hand-side of the road there is a small car park.
We leave through a gateway by a barrier by the National Trust sign labelled Ysgyryd Fawr.
We continue to reach a gate and a stile behind having a bench (phew, already!) and information board. Wrested, we continue, up steps into woodland known as Caer Wood

There are branching options, but, sadly, we must stay pretty straight, always going as steeply as possible uphill until we reach a fork. Here we take the Right-hand route even though it is the lower of the options. The Left-hand route is distinguished by steps; we'll use these on our descent a little later.
As we climb we can see hills on the Right. The one with the distinctive 'nipple' is Garway Hill. The nipple is the old RAF lookout point build for WWII, but seemingly never used. Garway Hill is the subject of a very good walk, too.
After about 1-mile we see a post for The Beacon's Way and from here we head straight up to attain the ridge.

We continue up the path (*The term 'path', we use rather loosely, here*)

37

ever upwards until we gain the Trig point and the ruined chapel of St Michael. *(…upping and upping until we reach the top of the hill)(Milne,1924)*

From here, we need map&compas and maybe thermos&sandwiches so that we can study and identify: to our north, Herefordshire and the Mendips; to our west the Brecon Beacons and the Black Mountains; to our South the Usk Valley and Somerset; and to our East Gloucestershire.

From here, following the Ridge takes us much of the way back to the car, after which we take a fairly short path through the woods to the steps down to the fork, passed earlier.
Thence we are allowed back to the car and rest!

From here the easiest and nearest post-perambulatory Real Ale is the Bell Inn in Skenfrith, with its fine dog&boot Bar.

Although this time I think I might make an exception and go a few minutes more to the Royal Arms in Llangrove.

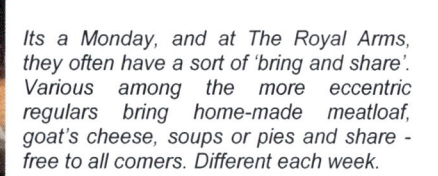

Its a Monday, and at The Royal Arms, they often have a sort of 'bring and share'. Various among the more eccentric regulars bring home-made meatloaf, goat's cheese, soups or pies and share - free to all comers. Different each week.

Today it's goat cheese and crackers; that'll do for me!

38

On the other hand, for completeness, you might drive to NP7 8DH, where you'll find the Skirrid Mountain Inn. Not so near as The Bell, but you just might think it an elegant formula. A fitting conclusion to your Skirrid exertions.

Wherever we decide to go, we'll have no good explanation for why we risked life & limb, not to say discomfort and exhaustion to climb (another!) mountain. All we can do is commiserate with each other and hope we'll never do it again!

The Kymin, Monmouth short walk

This is a 1/2-hour, circular, walk, not strenuous, with fine views. It takes us through woodland with a clear viewing point. Can be muddy!

(Or there is a 1½-hour strenuous walk, using Offa's Dyke.)

Take a compass, binoculars, a map and your stick.

Some walks take us over well-trodden paths where your heart-attack will see you discovered and revived in mere minutes. This is one such, unlike some, we know, that take us on *the path less Travelled* (Frost,1920) such that if you were eventually found it will be no more than your bleached bones that remain to decorate the scenery.

There is a free car park at the top of the hill, for the short walk; we're going that way, we're not mad.

We take the A4136, from The Monmouth traffic lights with the A40, cross the river bridge and go over the roundabout in the direction of Coleford. As we begin to climb up into the Forest, the road takes a bend to the left and there is a narrow lane on our right, signed The Kymin. This is Kymin Road and we follow it zigging and zagging to finally reach a grass car park on the left hand side of the road at the top of the hill.

We park and walk, ascending further, towards the white folly; the Naval Temple. Erected during The Napoleonic Wars and finished in 1801, this commemorates Admiral Lord Nelson and several other admirals I've never heard of. With stone wall and iron gates, its claiming to be the oldest monument to the Royal Navy.

We walk onwards to the Georgian Round House a few yards further on, built as a pleasant place to host a dining club, for days when pick nicks were made impossible by weather. The views from here over Monmouth town, and beyond are remarkable and it is worth taking a few minutes to identify all of the obvious buildings and streets. It is also possible to see Sugarloaf Mountain, a sort-of pointed volcano, and on a clear day *(Huh, this is Wales – we don't have many of those!)* Pen y Fan, the highest of the Brecon Beacons.

We continue along the drive. The ancient looking woodland is the Beaulieu Grove, which like so many woods hereabout was used for charcoal burning. We take a right turning before reaching the woods, proper. There is a stone cottage which was the stable for the diners' horses, and is now lived in by The Kymin's caretakers.

In front of the gates for the Old Stable, we turn left and follow a short path to a kissing gate. Through the gate, we take the smaller path to the left, reaching a fence between the field and Beaulieu Wood.

We follow the fence line where there are some pretty impressive wood ant hills. These are fine looking creatures, sometimes approaching ½-inch in length. If the ants are active, it is great to watch them; so industrious as they are. Ahead, through a gap in the trees, we might see the Malvern Hills.

We continue to the far left-hand corner of the field, where we turn right and follow a path to the next corner. Again, we turn right and follow a path leading diagonally back to the kissing gate used earlier. Nearing the gate, looking towards the Wye Valley (on our left), is *The Cathedral in the Forest* or Newland.Church.

We repass the kissing gate, with The Old Stable to our left, and reach the Bowling Green, landscaped as part of the Round House development. This all started life as a picnic area and it would seem wrong not to open a thermos flask and sandwich box, to toast the 19th Century builders.

As a very short additional section, we must return to the track by the Round House and follow the path through the heart of the wood for a few hundred yards to the end. This takes us nowhere, but these ancient woods have a fantastic atmosphere. We soak up the sheer antiquity of it all for a bit and then retrace our path to the car park.

Now, post-perambulatory ale.

We could try the inviting *(and having proximity!)* Mayhill Hotel,

or we could cross back over the river and the A40 and reach magnificent building that is the Queen's head Inn, in a beautiful medieval quarter of Monmouth town.

Both have merit.

We'll enjoy this beer; we only did the short route! Hurrah!!

41

The Kymin, Monmouth longer walk

This is a 1½-hour, pan-handle, walk, somewhat strenuous, with fine views. It takes us through woodland using a section of the ancient Offa's Dyke Path with a clear viewing point. Can be muddy!

Take a compass, binoculars, a map and your stick.

Some walks take us over well-trodden paths where your heart-attack will see you discovered and revived in mere minutes. this is one such, unlike some, we know, that take us on *the path less Travelled* (Frost,1920) such that if you were eventually found it will be no more than your bleached bones that remain to decorate the scenery.

We take the A4136, from The Monmouth traffic lights with the A40, cross the river bridge and reach a roundabout We park wherever is convenient here.

We walk a short way in the direction of Coleford and as we begin to climb up into the Forest, we see a track climbing off to the right of the road. This is one of those inviting tracks that we have seen from the car over many years and always wanted to walk. This is a part of the ancient Offa's Dyke Path

We ascend, sometimes using the lane *'Kymin Road'*, sometimes using the ancient Offa's Dyke Path, all signposted, towards the top, where there is the white folly that can be seen from the A40, for many miles in each direction. This is the 'Naval Temple'. Erected during The Napoleonic Wars and finished in 1801. This building commemorates Admiral Lord Nelson and several others. It has a low stone wall with ornamental iron gates, claiming to be the oldest monument to the Royal Navy that we have.

We walk onwards to the Georgian Round House a few yards further on, built as a pleasant place to host a dining club. The views from here over Monmouth town, and beyond are remarkable and it is worth taking a few minutes to identify all of the obvious buildings and streets. It is also possible to see Sugarloaf Mountain, a sort-of

42

pointed volcano, and on a clear day *(Ha Ha, this is Wales – we don't have many of those!)* Pen y Fan, the highest of the Brecon Beacons.

We continue along the drive. The ancient looking woodland is the Beaulieu Grove, which like so many woods hereabout was used for charcoal burning. We take a right turning before entering the woods, proper. The stone cottage was the stable for the diners' horses, and is now lived in by The Kymin's caretakers.

In front of the gates for the Old Stable, we turn left and follow a short path to a kissing gate. Through the gate, we take the smaller path to the left, reaching a fence between the field and Beaulieu Wood.

We follow the fence line where there are some pretty grand wood ant hills. These are impressive looking creatures, sometimes approaching ½-inch in length. If the ants are active, it is great to watch them; so industrious, they are. Ahead, through a gap in the trees, we might see the Malvern Hills.

We continue to the far left-hand corner of the field, where we turn right and follow a path to opposite corner. Again, we turn right and follow a path leading diagonally back to the kissing gate seen earlier. Nearing the gate, looking towards the Wye Valley (on our left), is *The Cathedral in the Forest* or Newland Church

We repass the kissing gate, with The Old Stable to our left, and reach the Bowling Green, landscaped as part of the Round House development. This all started life as a picnic area and it would seem wrong not to open a thermos flask and sandwich box, to toast the 19the century builders.

As a very short additional section, we return to the track by the Round House and follow the path through the heart of the wood for a few hundred yards to the end. This takes us nowhere, but these ancient woods have a fantastic atmosphere. We soak up the sheer antiquity of it all for a bit and then return towards the Folly until we see the Path on our right and retrace our route to the car. Going down is far easier and far quicker.

Now, post-perambulatory ale.

We could try the Mayhill Hotel

Or cross back over the river and the A40 and reach magnificent building that is the Queen's head Inn, in a beautiful medieval quarter of Monmouth town.

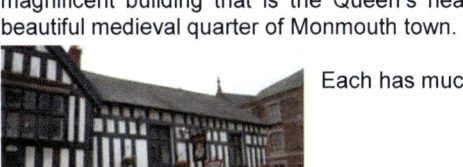

Each has much merit.

We'll enjoy this beer, but we'll feel dreadful for the first couple; we did the longer route! Oh no!! WHY?

43

Note: *This text is offered on the inventive new 'Createspace' Publishing platform for two reasons:*

1) *The costs to the reader are far lower than traditional publishing houses.*
2) *It is easy to update and improve the work; the text is continually under review. To this end the readers and the authors form a community to develop the work. As a reader, you are invited to email suggestions to nwheeler@brookes.ac.uk Contributions may be simple 'typo' alerts, corrections to detail, new areas to cover, etc. All contributors are acknowledged in the print and E-Book versions, with our thanks.*

*We walk up the hill, As, ever, we will,
And we scramble and amble, With endless preamble,
And talk a good outin',Of high hill and of mou'tain,
And glory in views; (More fun than The News.)
It does do you good, Well, you knew that it would.
So we top the corona: The mountain's persona,
Is always a thrill, And always it will,
Take your breath and excite, As we thought that it might.
And the aerial view, Of the bar: with that stew,
Just calls to your heart, So downwards we start,
On the path to nutrition. The staff to petition,
A plate; Yes that's great! I've a hunger to sate
And a little more bread, Though, I know what I said.
I'm watching my weight, But we set out at eight!
We deserve a good meal, So a rich stew, I feel,
Is just what we've earned, With those calories burned,
As we sit to consume, The food, we assume,
That it's goat or lamb? It's surely not ham?
And I can tell you that, I'll be guarding my cat!
I'm thinking of saying, More words, but you're praying,*

I'll stop; so I will.

Printed in Great Britain
by Amazon